Jacob of Serugh

Analecta Gorgiana

1051

Series Editor

George Anton Kiraz

Analecta Gorgiana is a collection of long essays and short monographs which are consistently cited by modern scholars but previously difficult to find because of their original appearance in obscure publications. Carefully selected by a team of scholars based on their relevance to modern scholarship, these essays can now be fully utilized by scholars and proudly owned by libraries.

Jacob of Serugh

A Select Bibliographical Guide

Sebastian P. Brock

gorgias press
2011

Gorgias Press LLC, 954 River Road, Piscataway, NJ, 08854, USA

www.gorgiaspress.com

Copyright © 2011 by Gorgias Press LLC

Originally published in 2010

All rights reserved under International and Pan-American Copyright Conventions. No part of this publication may be reproduced, stored in a retrieval system or transmitted in any form or by any means, electronic, mechanical, photocopying, recording, scanning or otherwise without the prior written permission of Gorgias Press LLC.

2011

ISBN 978-1-4632-0099-2 **ISSN 1935-6854**

Reprinted from the 2010 Piscataway edition.

Printed in the United States of America

JACOB OF SERUGH:
A SELECT BIBLIOGRAPHICAL GUIDE

SEBASTIAN BROCK

ABBREVIATIONS

Assemani = Assemani, J.S. *Bibliotheca Orientalis*, I, 305–39. Rome, 1719; repr. Piscataway NJ, 2002 (numbered list of Jacob's *Mimrē*)

Albert, *Homélies* = Albert, M. *Homélies contres les juifs par Jacques de Saroug.* Patrologia Orientalis, 38:1; 1976.

Albert, *Lettres* = Albert, M. *Les Lettres de Jacques de Saroug.* Patrimoine syriaque, 3. Kaslik, 2004.

Alwan = Alwan, Kh. *Jacques de Saroug, Quatre homélies métriques sur la création.* CSCO, 508, Scr. Syri, 214–5; 1989.

B = Bedjan, P. *Homiliae Selectae Mar-Jacobi Sarugensis*, I–V. Paris/Leipzig, 1905–1910; repr. I–VI, Piscataway, 2006. Cited by volume, page and homily number; vol. VI of the reprint contains the eleven memre published by Bedjan at the end of his *Martyrii qui et Sahdona quae supersunt*, 603–85.[1] Paris/Leipzig, 1902, together with five further memre.

BA = Bedjan, P. *Acta Martyrum et Sanctorum* I–VII. Paris/Leipzig, 1890–97.

Bickell = Bickell, G. *Ausgewählte Gedichte der Syrischen Kirchenväter.* Kempten, 1872.

---

[1] The first nine of these were also published separately by Bedjan, P. *Cantus seu Homiliae Mar-Jacobi in Jesum et Mariam*, Paris/Leipzig, 1902; B VI retains both paginations.

[Most of these translations also appear in Landersdorfer, and so are not mentioned further below].

ET = English translation.

Frothingham = Frothingham, A.L. "L'Omelia di Giacomo di Sarug sul battesimo di Costantino imperatore." *Atti della R. Accademia dei Lincei* (Anno CCLXXIX, 1881–2), ser. 3. *Memorie della Classe di Scienze morali, storiche e filologiche* 8 (1882): 167–242.

FT = French translation.

GT = German translation.

Guidi = Guidi, I. "Testi orientali inediti sopra i sette dormienti di Efeso." *Reale Accademia dei Lincei* (Anno CCLXXXII, 1884–85), Ser. 3. *Memorie della Classe di Scienze morali, storiche et filologiche* 12 (1884): 1–105 (esp. 18–19). (Anno CCLXXXII, 1884–85): 18–29.

Hansbury = Hansbury, M. *Jacob of Serug, On the Mother of God*. Crestwood NY, 1998.

Isabaert-Cauuet = Isabaert-Cauuet, I. *Jacques de Saroug, Homélies sur la Fin du Monde*. Paris, 2005.

IT = Italian translation.

Kollamparampil = Kollamparampil, T. *Jacob of Serugh, Select Festal Homilies*. Rome/Bangalore, 1997.

Landersdorfer = Landersdorfer, S. *Ausgewählte Schriften der Syrischen Dichter*. Kempten, 1912.

LT = Latin translation.

MHMJS = *The Metrical Homilies of Mar Jacob of Sarug*. Piscataway, NJ, 2008–.

Mouterde = Mouterde, P. "Deux homélies inédites de Jacques de Saroug." *Mélanges de l'Université Saint Joseph* 26 (1944/6): 1–56.

Overbeck = Overbeck, J.J. *S. Ephraemi Syri, Rabbulae episcopi Balaei aliorumque opera selecta*. Oxford, 1865.

Reinink = Reinink, G.J. *Das syrische Alexanderlied in drei Rezensionen*. CSCO, 454–5; Scr. Syri, 195–6; 1983.

SM = Brock, S.P., ed. *Soghyatha mgabbyatha*. Monastery of St Ephrem, Holland, 1982.

Strothmann, *Thomas* = *Jakob von Sarug: drei Gedichte über den Apostel Thomas*. Göttinger Orientforschungen, Reihe Syriaca, 12; 1976.

Vona = Vona, C. *Omilie Mariologiche di S. Giacomo di Sarug*. Rome, 1953.

Vööbus, *Handschriftliche Überlieferung* = Vööbus, A. *Handschriftliche Überlieferung der Memre-Dichtung des Ja'qob von Serug*, I–IV. CSCO, 344–5, 421–2 = Sub. 39–40, 60–1; 1973, 1980.

INTRODUCTION

The contents of all five volumes of Paul Bedjan's edition of the *Mimre*/Homilies, together with those in the added volume VI of the reprint (Piscataway NJ, 2006), can readily be found in vol. VI, pp. xiii–xxi. Also in VI, pp. 372–99, a list of incipits is provided; this includes not only published *mimre*, but also unpublished ones, insofar as this information is available in catalogues.[2] The standard guide to the manuscripts is Vööbus, *Handschriftliche Überlieferung*, I–IV; a listing of those used by Bedjan is given in vol. VI, 407–9. Fuller bibliographies on Jacob are indicated in III.4, below.

I. JACOB'S WORKS, BY GENRE AND TOPIC

I.1. *Mimre*

It has been possible to derive the topics (and first lines) for a number of unpublished *mimre* from Assemani and from Mar Filoksinos Yohanna Dolabany, *Catalogue of Syriac Manuscripts in Za'faran Monastery* (ed. Mar Gregorios Yohanna Ibrahim; Syriac Patrimony, 9; 1994), pp.45–58 (entry on the huge twelfth-century manuscript which is now Damascus, Syrian Orthodox Patriarchate ms 12/15).

(a) Old Testament

Aaron: Hom. 5 (B I, 68–84). FT by M. Wurmbrand in *L'Orient Syrien* 6 (1961): 255–78.

---

[2] An earlier version of this, but also including *mimre* by Narsai and Isaac of Antioch, was published in my "The published verse homilies of Isaac of Antioch, Jacob of Serugh, and Narsai: index of incipits," *Journal of Semitic Studies* 32 (1987): 279–313.

Abraham and Isaac: unpublished.

Abraham and his Types: Hom. 109 (B IV, 61–103). ET by R.E. McCarron, in *Hugoye* 1:1 (1998), and by E. Thelly, in *The Harp* 24 (2009): 179–88.

Adam, Creation of, and Resurrection of the Dead: Hom. 72 (B III, 152–7), and Alwan IV (with FT).

Adam, created mortal or immortal?: ed. with FT, Alwan II.

Adam's Expulsion from Paradise: ed. with FT, Alwan, III.

Asa, king: unpublished.

Azaza'el:—see Two Goats.

Babel, Tower of: Hom. 33 (B II, 1–27). Text and ET by A.M. Butts, in MHMJS 15 (2009).

Balaam and Balak: unpublished.

Bronze Serpent: Hom. 4 (B I, 49–67). ET in *The True Vine* 6 (1990): 38–56.

Cain and Abel (I): Hom. 147 (B V, 1–16).

Cain and Abel (II): Hom. 148 (B V, 17–32).

Cain and Abel (III): Hom. 149 (B V, 32–47).

Cain, Abel and Seth: Hom. 150 (B V, 47–61).

Creation, Six Days of:

First Day: Hom. 71.1 (B III, 1–27). ET by R.D. Young in Trigg, J.W., ed. *Message of the Fathers of the Church IX*, 184–202. Wilmington, 1988.

Second Day: Hom. 71.2 (B III, 27–43).

Third Day: Hom. 71.2 (B III, 43–60).

Fourth Day: Hom. 71.4 (B III, 60–79).

Fifth Day: Hom. 71.5 (B III, 79–97).

Sixth Day: Hom. 71.6 (B III, 97–129). FT by B. Sony, in *Parole de l'Orient* 11 (1983): 172–99.

Seventh Day: Hom. 71.7 (B III, 129–51).

Text and Arabic translation, with studies by Sony, B. *L'Homélie de Jacques de Saroug sur l'Hexaméron*, I–II. Rome, 2000. For a study, see T. Jansma, in *L'Orient Syrien* 4 (1959): 3–42, 129–62, 253–284.

Daniel (I) and Nebuchadnezzar's Dream: Hom. 123 (B IV, 491–516). (For the supplementation of part of a lacuna, see *Parole de l'Orient* 13 (1986): 84–5, 89–90).

Daniel (III) and the Tree which Nebuchadnezzar saw: Hom. 124 (B IV, 517–43). ET by M. Henze, in his *The Madness of King*

Nebuchadnezzar. The Ancient Near Eastern Origins and Early History of Interpretation of Daniel 4, 251–69. Leiden, 1999.

Daniel and Three Companions in the Furnace: Hom. 36 (B II, 94–137).

David and Goliath: Hom. 34 (B II, 28–76). On this *mimro* see C.E. Morrison, in Kiraz, G., ed. *Malphono w-Rabo d-Malphone*, 477–96. Piscataway, NJ, 2008.

David and Uriah: Hom. 162 (B V, 367–93). On this *mimro* see A.G. Salvesen, in Kiraz, G., ed. *Malphono w-Rabo d-Malphone*, 568–72. Piscataway, NJ, 2008.

David: unpublished.

Elijah (I–V): Edition and ET by S.A. Kaufman, in MHMJS 9–13 (2009).

Elijah (II), his Flight from Jezebel: Hom. 112 (B IV, 133–54). FT of Homs 112–15 by F. Graffin and others in *Le Saint Prophète Élie d'après les Pères de l'Église*, 484–604. Spiritualité Orientale, 53; 1992.

Elijah (III) and Naboth: Hom. 113 (B IV, 154–207).

Elijah (IV) and king Ahaziah: Hom. 114 (B IV, 207–26).

Elijah (V), his Ascent to Heaven: Hom. 115 (B IV, 226–60).

Elisha, (I): Hom. 116 (B IV, 261–81). FT of Homs 116–21 and 35 by F. Graffin and others in *Le Saint Prophète Élisée d'après les Pères de l'Église*, 249–363, 365–82. Spiritualité Orientale, 59; 1993. Edition and ET of Elisha I–VII by S.A. Kaufman, in MHMJS (forthcoming).

Elisha (II) and the king of Moab: Hom. 117 (B IV, 282–96). ET in *The True Vine* 1 (1989): 51–67.

Elisha (III) and the Shunamite Woman: Hom. 118 (B IV, 296–317).

Elisha (IV) and Naaman and Gehazi: Hom. 119 (B IV, 318–32).

Elisha (V) and the Vision of the Saints: Hom. 120 (B IV, 333–49).

Elisha (VI) and the Capture of Samaria: Hom. 121 (B IV, 349–67).

Elisha's bones which raised a dead person: Hom. 35 (B II, 77–94).

Ezekiel's Vision of the dry Bones: unpublished.

Ezekiel's Vision of the Chariot: Hom. 125 (B IV, 543–610). On this *mimro* see A. Golitzin, in *St Vladimir's Theological Quarterly* 46:2–3 (2003): 323–64, repr. in *Scrinium* 3 (2003): 180–212.

Ezekiel's Vision of the Torrent: Hom. 164 (B V, 430–47).

Flood: Hom. 108 (B IV, 1–61).

Gen. 1:26 and Nativity: ed. with FT, Alwan I.

Hosea: ed. + GT by Strothmann, W. *Jakob von Sarug: der Prophet Hosea*. Göttinger Orientforschungen, Reihe Syriaca, 5; 1973.

Isaac's Blessings on Jacob: Hom. 73 (B III, 175–91).

Isaiah and king Uzziah: Hom. 163 (B V, 393–429).

Isaiah 9:6: unpublished.

Jacob, Rachel, Leah; Christ, the Church and the Synagogue: Hom. 75 (B III, 208–23). ET in *The True Vine* 4:4 (1993): 50–64.

Jacob's Revelation at Bethel: Hom. 74 (B III, 192–207). FT by F. Graffin in *L'Orient Syrien* 5 (1960): 227–46. GT in Landersdorfer, 332–43. On this *mimro* see C. Lange, in *The Harp* 20 (2006): 209–20.

Jacob's Rods: unpublished.

Jephtha's Daughter: Hom. 159 (B V, 306–30). ET by S.A. Harvey (forthcoming).

Job: Hom. 157 (B V, 202–89).

Jonah and Nineveh: Hom. 122 (B IV, 368–490). On this *mimro* see R. Kitchen, in *Hugoye* 11:1 (2008), and in Kiraz, G., ed. *Malphono w-Rabo d-Malphone*, 365–81. Piscataway, NJ, 2008.

Joseph 1–10: unpublished.

Joshua 1–2: unpublished.

Lawgiver of Old and New Testament is the same: Hom. 136 (B IV, 803–17).

Melkizedek: Hom. 155 (B V, 154–80). ET in *The True Vine* 2 (1989): 30–55.

Melkizedek, 'You are a priest for ever': Hom. 41 (B II, 197–209). ET by J. Thekeparampil in *The Harp* 6 (1993): 53–64. On Melkizedek in Jacob, see Thekeparampil in Lavenant, R., ed. *VI Symposium Syriacum*, 121–33. Orientalia Christiana Analecta, 247; 1994.

Moses and Amalek: unpublished.

Moses, Burial of: unpublished.

Moses and Burning Bush: unpublished.

Moses and Exodus: unpublished.

Moses' Extended Hands: Hom. 158 (B V, 290–306).

___ : unpublished.

Moses and Manna: unpublished.

Moses and the Rock: unpublished.

Moses' Veil: Hom. 79 (B III, 283–305). Text and ET by S.P. Brock in MHMJS 1 (2009), and ET in *Sobornost/Eastern Churches Review* 3 (1981): 72–84, repr. in *Studies in Syriac Spirituality*, 177–

209. Bangalore, 2008. FT by P. Mouterde, in *Dieu Vivant* 12 (1948): 49–62, and by J. Babakhan, in *La Vie Spirituelle* 91 (1954): 142–56. Dutch tr. by Welkenhuysen, A. *De Sluier van Mozes*. Brugge, 1983; 3rd edn 1994.

Moses and Water of Marah: unpublished.

Moses' Words 'The Lord will raise up for you a prophet like me': Hom. 110 (B IV, 104–16).

Moses and Consecration of the Church: Hom. 3 (B I, 38–48).

Moses : unpublished.

Passover of the Law and Thursday of Mysteries:—see below.

Philistines: unpublished.

Phineas: unpublished.

Psalm 148: Hom. 106 (B III, 892–906).

Rebecca, Betrothal of: unpublished. Excerpts, and FT by F. Graffin, *L'Orient Syrien* 3 (1958): 324–36.

Red Heifer: Hom. 77 (B III, 242–59). ET by D.J. Lane, in *The Harp* 15 (2002): 25–42. Study by P. Zingerle, in *Zeitschrift für katholische Theologie* 11 (1887): 92–108.

Samson (I): Hom. 160 (B V, 331–55). ET in *The True Vine* 11 (1992): 51–70.

Samson (II): Hom. 161 (B V, 355–67).

Sinai, Descent of the Most High on: Hom. 2 (B I, 3–38). FT by Babakan, *Revue de l'Orient Chrétien* 17 (1912), 411–26; 18 (1913), 42–52.

Sodom (I): Hom 151 (B V, 61–77).

Sodom (II): Hom. 152 (B V, 78–96).

Sodom (III): Hom. 153 (B V, 96–116).

Sodom (IV): Hom. 154 (B V, 117–53)

Solomon's Judgement: Hom. 111 (B IV, 116–32). Text and ET in S.A. Kaufman, *MHMJS* 4 (2008).

Tamar and Judah: B VI, 255–69. ET by S.P. Brock, in *Le Muséon* 115 (2002): 293–302.

Two Goats: Hom. 78 (B III, 259–83). ET by D.J. Lane, in *The Harp* 18 (2005): 365–91.

Two Sparrows in the Law: Hom. 76 (B III, 224–42). FT by F. Graffin, in *L'Orient Syrien* 6 (1961): 54–66.

Uzzah: unpublished.

'Vanity of Vanities': Hom. 104 (B III, 858–75). GT by Deppe, K. *Kohelet in der syrischen Dichtung*, 68–121. Göttinger Orientforschungen, Reihe Syriaca, 6; 1975.

(b) New Testament

Annunciation:—see (c).
'Are you the one who comes?': unpublished.
'Behold, we have left everything': Hom. 59 (B II, 689–704).
Cherub and the Repentant Thief: Hom.177 (B V, 658–87).
Christ's Combat with Satan (I): Hom 82 (B III, 335–63).
Christ's Combat with Satan (II): Hom. 126 (B IV, 610–31).
Christ portrayed as Food and Drink: Hom. 43 (B II, 228–244).
Christ's Thirty Years before Miracles: Hom. 81 (B III, 321–34). ET in *The True Vine* 4 (1990): 37–49.
Christ walking on Water: unpublished.
Christ as incomprehensible: unpublished.
Christ's body passible before the Resurrection: unpublished.
Coin in the Fish: unpublished.
Crucifixion: see (c).
Emmanuel: Hom. 40 (B II, 184–96).
Fig Tree cursed: Hom. 132 (B IV, 724–39).
Galatians 6:14: unpublished.
'In the Beginning was the Word': Hom. 38 (B II, 158–69).
Innocents, Slaughter of: unpublished.
Lazarus, Resurrection of: Hom. 93 (B III, 564–81).
Magi, Star of, and Slaughter of Innocents: Hom. 6 (B I, 84–152).
Mary:—see (c) and (e).

Miracles:
Canaanite Woman healed: Hom. 17 (B I, 424–44).
Centurion's son healed: Hom. 45 (B II, 265–80).
Deaf, Blind and Possessed, healing of: unpublished.
Five Loaves and Two Fishes: Hom. 87 (B III, 425–62).
Jairus' Daughter healed: Hom, 91 (B III, 530–45).
___: unpublished.
Lame Man healed by Peter and John: Hom. 179 (B V, 708–31).
Leper healed: Hom. 44 (B II, 244–64).
Man possessed by Legion healed: Hom. 130 (B IV, 683–700).
Paralytic aged 38 healed: Hom. 131 (B IV, 701–24).
Paralytic healed: unpublished.
Three Dead Persons raised: Hom. 48 (B II, 334–47).
Timaeus' blindness healed: Hom. 88 (B III, 462–83).
Wedding at Cana: Hom. 167 (B V, 480–94). GT by S. Grill in *Jahrbuch der Österreichischen Byzantinischen Gesellschaft* 8 (1959): 17–28.

Widow of Nain's Son raised: Hom. 92 (B III, 546–63).
___: unpublished.
Woman bent double, healing of: Hom. 169 (B V, 506–25).
Woman with affliction, healing of: Hom. 170 (B V, 525–51).
Only-Begotten Word: Hom 39 (B II, 169–84).
Parables:
Camel and the Rich Man: Hom. 128 (B IV, 649–66).
Feast made by King for his Son: Hom. 171 (B V, 551–69).
Five Talents: Hom. 173 (B V, 587–613).
Good Samaritan: Hom. 47 (B II, 312–33).
Kingdom of Heaven as Leaven: Hom. 86 (B III, 411–34). ET in *The True Vine* 3 (1989): 44–57.
Kingdom of Heaven as a Mustard Seed: Hom. 127 (B IV, 632–49).
Loaves and Fishes: Hom. 87 (B III, 425–62).
Lost Coin and lost Sheep: unpublished.
Pharisee and Tax Collector: Hom. 13 (B I, 299–319). ET in *The True Vine* 9 (1991), 19–34.
Prodigal Son: Hom. 12 (B I, 267–99). ET in *The True Vine* 5:4 (1994), 11–37.
___: Hom. 90 (B III, 500–29).
Rich Man and Lazarus: Hom. 16 (B I, 364–424).
Ten Virgins: Hom. 50 (B II, 375–401). ET in *The True Vine* 4:1 (1992): 39–62.
Treasure hidden in a field: Hom. 168 (B V, 494–506).
Vineyard: Hom. 133 (B IV, 740–66).
Wedding Garment: unpublished.
Woman with Seven Husbands: Hom. 172 (B V, 569–87).
Workers in the Vineyard: Hom. 14 (B I, 320–44).
Repentant Thief: Hom. 52 (B II, 428–46).
Samaritan Woman: Hom. 46 (B II, 281–312).
Signs performed by Christ: Hom. 129 (B IV, 666–83).
Simon Peter, Denial of: Hom. 21 (B I, 506–31).
Sinful Woman: Hom. 51 (B II, 402–28). ET by S.F. Johnson, *Sobornost/Eastern Churches Review* 24 (2002): 56–88.
Synagogue, adultery of: unpublished.
Third Resurrection Appearance: Hom. 178 (B V, 687–707).
'This one is appointed for Fall and Uprising of Many': Hom. 166 (B V, 467–80).
Two Thieves: unpublished.

Types and Symbols of Christ: Hom. 80 (B III, 305–21). For this cento, see J. Konat, in *Le Muséon* 118 (2005): 71–86.

Widow with Two Small Coins: Hom. 89 (B III, 483–500).

Words of Christ:

Beatitudes: Hom. 83 (B III, 363–74).

'Do not swear at all': Hom. 84 (B III, 375–95).

'Foxes have holes': Hom. 85 (B III, 411–24).

'Get thee behind me, Satan': Hom. 20 (B I, 482–506). Text with ET by A.C. McCollum, in MHMJS 22 (2009).

'Our Father...': Hom. 10 (B I, 212–48).

'Seek what is above...': Hom. 105 (B III, 876–92).

'What will it profit a person...': Hom. 30 (B I, 683–98).

'Who do people say I am?: Hom.19 (B I, 460–82). GT in Landersdorfer, 316–32.

Zacchaeus the Tax Collector: Hom. 15 (B I, 344–64).

Zacharias:—see (c).

(c) Liturgical Year

Zachariah, Annunciation to: Hom. 37 (B II, 137–58).

Mary, Annunciation to: B VI, 27–49. ET in Hansbury, 43–64. IT in Vona, 135–50.

___: ed. with ET by A. Shemunkasho, in Kiraz, G., ed. *Malphono w-rabo d-Malphone*.

___: unpublished.

Visitation of Mary to Elizabeth: B VI, 49–73. ET in Hansbury, 65–88. IT in Vona, 151–67.

Nativity (I): B VI, 108–62. ET in Kollamparampil, 37–93.

Nativity (II): B VI, 163–78. ET in Kollamparampil, 94–107.

Nativity: B VI, 178–96. ET in Kollamparampil, 108–27.

Nativity: unpublished.

Epiphany (Baptism of Christ): Hom. 8 (B I, 167–93). ET in Kollamparampil, 159–86, and MHMJS 2 (2008).

Presentation: Hom. 165 (B V, 447–66). ET in Kollamparampil, 138–58.

Great Fast (I): Hom. 23 (B I, 551–70).

Great Fast (II), Hom. 24 (B I, 571–87).

Great Fast (III): Hom. 25 (B I, 588–606).

Palm Sunday (Hosannas): Hom. 18 (B I, 445–59). ET in Kollamparampil, 246–60, and MHMJS 3 (2008).

Monday of Hosannas: Hom. 174 (B V, 613–31).

Holy Week:
1. Monday: Hom. 53.1 (B II, 447–70).
2. Tuesday, Vigil: Hom. 53.2 (B II, 470–88).
3. Wednesday, Vigil: Hom. 53.3 (B II, 489–504).
4. Thursday, Vigil: Hom. 53.4 (B II, 505–21).
5. Friday, Vigil: Hom. 53.5 (B II, 522–54).
6. Friday of Passion: Hom. 53.6 (B II, 554–79). ET of excerpts by R.H. Connolly, *The Downside Review* 27 (1908): 285–7.
7. Saturday, Vigil: Hom. 53.6 (B II, 580–98).
8. Sunday, Vigil: Hom. 53.7 (B II, 598- 610).

Thursday of the Mysteries: Hom. 175 (B V, 631–41).

Friday of the Passion

Penitent Thief: Hom. 52 (B II, 428–46). GT in Landersdorfer, 360–74.

Two Thieves: unpublished.

Cherub and Thief: Hom. 177 (B V, 658–87). GT of excerpts by Zingerle, *Theologische Quartalschrift* 53 (1871): 417–420.

Descent to Sheol: unpublished.

Death and Satan: Hom.176 (B V, 641–58).

Burial of Christ: unpublished.

Resurrection: Hom. 54 (B II, 611–23). ET in Kollamparampil, 292–305, and MHMJS 5 (2008).

Resurrection: Hom. 55 (B II, 624–35). ET in Kollamparampil, 306–17, and Kollamparampil in MHMJS 5 (2008).

New Sunday: Hom. 57 (B II, 649–69). ET in *The True Vine* 4:2 (1992), 49–66.

Ascension: B VI, 196–220. ET in Kollamparampil, 329–52.

Pentecost: Hom. 58 (B II, 670–89). ET in Kollamparampil, 353–69. GT in Landersdorfer, 271–85.

Transfiguration: Hom. 49 (B II, 347–75). ET in Kollamparampil, 201–30, and MHMJS 8 (2008). FT by E. Khoury, *Parole de l'Orient* 15 (1988/9), 65–90.

(d) Other liturgical

Baptisms, the Three: Hom. 7 (B I, 153–67). See (f), under Three Baptisms.

Burial of Strangers: ed. with FT, by P. Mouterde, in *Mélanges de l'Université Saint Joseph* 26 (1944/6): 15–22.

Consecration of Church: Hom. 134 (B IV, 767–89). GT by Grill, S. *Jakob von Sarug. Die Kirche und die Forschung.* Heiligenkreuzer Studien, 13; 1963.

Myron, consecration of (also attributed to George bp of the Arab tribes):[3] Ryssel, V., ed. *Poemi siriaci di Giorgio, vescovo degli Arabi*, 48–80. Atti, Accademia dei Lincei, Cl. Sc.Mor., Stor. et Filol., IV.9; 1892. GT by Ryssel, V. *Georgs des Araberbischofs Gedichte und Briefe*, 14–36. Leipzig, 1891.

Mysteries, reception of: Hom. 95 (B III, 646–63). Text and ET by A. Harrak, in MHMJS 17 (2009). ET of excerpts by R.H. Connolly, in *The Downside Review* 27 (1908): 278–87. FT by J. van der Ploeg, in *Studi e Testi* 233 (1964): 401–18.

Praise at Morning and Evening: Hom. 107 (B III, 907–12). ET in *The True Vine* 7:2 (1998): 59–64.

Praise at Table, 1–8: Homs 139–46 (B IV, 872–914).

(e) Saints

Abhai: unpublished.
Addai: unpublished.
Apostles: unpublished.
Bacchus: BA VI, 650–61.
Barsauma: unpublished.
Behnam: unpublished.
Confessors and Martyrs: Hom. 56 (B II, 636–49).
Constantine, Baptism of: B VI, 297–323. IT in Frothingham, 33–52. On this *mimro* see M. Kohlbacher, in Tamcke, M., ed. *Syriaca*, 29–76. Münster, 2002.
Dimet: unpublished.
Ephesus, Sleepers of: B VI, 324–30. ET by S.P. Brock, in Allen, P., and others, eds. *Festschrift for Michael Lattke*, 13–30. Early Christian Studies, 12. Strathfield, NSW, 2007. LT by Benedictus, P. *Acta Sanctorum Julii VI*, 387–8. Antwerp, 1729. Ed. and IT of expanded recension in I. Guidi, 29–32.

---

[3] The mimro is attributed to Jacob in Damascus, Patr. 12/15 (no. 102) and in several other manuscripts.

Ephrem: BA III, 665–79; better edition by Amar, PO, 47:1; 1995, with ET.
George: Hom. 181 (B V, 747–70).
Gurya:—see under Shmona.
Habbib: BA I, 160–72. ET by Cureton, W. *Ancient Syriac Documents*, 86–96. London, 1864, and by R. Doran in Valentasis, R. *Religions in Late Antiquity*, 413–23. Princeton, 2000.
Helena: see Cross, finding of (in (f) below).
John the Baptist, Praises of: Hom. 97 (B III, 687–710). FT of excerpts by J. Babakan, *Revue de l'Orient Chrétien* 19 (1914): 150–3.
John the Baptist, Beheading of: Hom. 96 (B III, 664–87). Abbreviated FT by Babakan in *Revue de l'Orient Chrétien* 19 (1914): 67–8, 1434–8.
John the Evangelist: Hom. 60 (B II, 705–16).
Juliana Saba: unpublished.
Laurentios: unpublished.
Martyrs: Hom. 56 (B II, 636–49); also attributed to Narsai).
Martyrs, Forty (of Sebaste): BA VI, 662–73.
Mary:[4] B VI, 2–27. ET in *True Vine* 5:1 (1994), 2–28, and in Hansbury, 17–42. GT in Landersdorfer, 285–303. IT in Vona, 115–34. LT in Abbeloos, 202–53.
Mary, her Virginity: B VI, 73–96. ET in Puthuparampil, J. *The Mariological Thought of Mar Jacob of Serugh*. Moran Etho, 25; 2005, Appendix, i–xxi. IT in Vona, 169–85. LT in Abbeloos, 256–301.
Mary and Golgotha: ed. with FT, by P. Mouterde, in *Mélanges de l'Université Saint Joseph* 26 (1944/6): 9–14.
Mary, her Death: B VI, 97–107. ET in Hansbury, 89–100, and by Shoemaker, S.J. *Ancient Traditions of the Virgin Mary's Dormition and Assumption*, 408–14. Oxford, 2002; IT by Vona, 187–94. LT by A. Baumstark, *Oriens Christianus* 5 (1905): 91–99.
Paul: Hom. 62 (B II, 747–69). ET in *The True Vine* 10 (1991): 57–73.
Paul, Conversion of: Hom. 61, (B II, 717–47)

---

[4] Many excerpts on Mary, drawn from Jacob's *mimre*, are to be found in Bedjan, P. *Mois de Marie*, 1–57, Pairs/Leipzig, 1904.

Paul, Peter and John at Antioch: B VI, 270–96. ET by Thomas, L.A.R. *The Legend concerning Peter at Antioch in Syriac Tradition*. BLitt. Diss. Oxford, 1978.
Saint, any: unpublished.
Sergius: BA VI, 650–61.
Sharbel: Moesinger, *Monumenta Syriaca* II, 52–63. Innsbruck, 1878.
Shmona: BA I, 131–43. ET by Cureton, W. *Ancient Syriac Documents*, 96–106. London, 1864; GT in Landersdorfer, 374–86.
Shmoni and her 7 children (Maccabees): unpublished.
Simeon the Stylite: BA IV, 650–65. ET by S.A. Harvey, in Wimbush, V.L., ed. *Ascetic Behavior in Graeco-Roman Antiquity*, 15–38. Minneapolis, 1990. FT (from GT) by Blersch, H.G. *La colonne au carrefour du monde*. Spiritualité Orientale, 77; 2001. GT in Landersdorfer, 387–405. IT by I. Pizzi, in *Bessarione* III.4 (Anno 12, 1908): 18–29. See also S.A. Harvey, in *Aram* 5 (1993): 219–41.
Stephen: Hom. 98 (B III, 710–23). ET in *The True Vine* 7 (1990): 43–54.
Theodore: unpublished.
Thomas I: Hom. 99 (B III, 724–62). GT in Strothmann, *Thomas*, 27–163.
Thomas II: ed. with GT in Strothmann, *Thomas*, 165–289.
Thomas, Palace in air: Hom. 100 (B III, 763–94); GT of short recension by R. Schröter, in *Zeitschrift der deutschen morgenländischen Gesellschaft* 25 (1871): 40–65, 321–77; cf 28 (1874): 584–626; ed. with GT of long recension in Strothmann, *Thomas*, 291–447.

(f) Other topics

Abgar: see Addai in (e).
Admonition: Hom. 1 (B I, 1–2).
Admoition: Hom. 182 (B V, 771–84).
Admonition: unpublished.
Alexander the Great: ed. with GT, G.J. Reinink, CSCO, 454–5; Scr.Syri, 195–6; 1983, replacing older editions.
Amid, sack of: unpublished.
Assembly of Bishops: unpublished.
Blasphemers, against: unpublished.

Body and Soul: SM 95–102. GT by H.J.W. Drijvers, in Reinink, G.J., and H.L.J. Vanstiphout, eds. *Dispute Poems and Dialogues*, 121–34. Orientalia Lovaniensia Analecta, 42; 1991.

Chalcedon, Council of: B VI, 331–37. ET by S.P. Brock in Abp Methodios, ed., *Texts and Studies* (Athens) 8/10 (1989/91): 448–59; FT by G. Krüger in *L'Orient Syrien* 2 (1957): 125–36.

Choice foods: unpublished.

Consolation: BA VI, 674–89.

Cross, finding of: unpublished.

Day and Night, Work and Rest: unpublished.

Departed bishops: unpublished.

Departed priests: unpublished.

Departed deacons: unpublished.

Departed monks: unpublished.

Departed strangers: unpublished.

Departed *bnat qyama*: Hom. 191 (B V, 821–36). On this *mimro* see R.A. Kitchen, in *Hugoye* 7:2 (2004).

Departed children: Hom. 189 (B V, 804–16).

Departed, Commoration of: Hom. 22 (B I, 535–50 = BA V, 615–627). ET by R.H. Connolly, in *The Downside Review* 29 (1910): 262–70, and Anon. in *The True Vine* 5 (1990): 41–53. GT in Landersdorfer, 304–15. Spanish tr. (< GT) in *Textos eucaristicos primitivos* II, 563–71. Madrid, 1954.

Departed: Hom. 69 (B II, 873–77).

Departed: Hom. 183 (B V, 781–4). Partial GT by Zingerle, *Zeitschrift der deutschen morgenländischen Gesellschaft* 20 (1866): 521–6. IT by G. Rinaldi, *Aevum* 22 (1948): 88–90.

Departed: unpublished.

Disputers: unpublished.

Edessa and Jerusalem: Hom. 180 (B V, 731–47). GT by P. Bruns, in Arnzen, R., and Thielmann, J., eds. *Words, Texts and Concepts*, 537–53. OLA 139; 2004.

End: Homs 31–2 (B I, 698–713, 713–20). FT in Isabaert-Cauuet, 17–50.

___: Homs 67–8 (B II, 836–58, 858–72). FT in Isabaert-Cauuet, 51–103.

___: Homs 192–5 (B V, 836–99). FT in Isabaert-Cauuet, 105–96. FT of Hom. 194 by Babakan in *Revue de l'Orient Chrétien* 18 (1913): 358–74.

___: unpublished.

Faith: Hom. 94 (B III, 581–646). GT of excerpts by G. Krüger, in *Ostkirchliche Studien* 23 (1974): 188–96.

___: unpublished.

Fall of idols: Hom. 101 (B III, 795–823). FT by J.P.P. Martin, in *Zeitschrift der deutschen morgenländischen Gesellschaft* 29 (1876): 107–47. GT in Landersdorfer, 406–31.

Hour of Death: unpublished.

Jews, against the: 7 homilies, ed. with FT, M. Albert. PO, 38; 1976.

Kingdom and Gehenna: unpublished.

Locusts, plague of: unpublished.

Love: Hom. 26 (B I, 606–27). ET by Anon. in *James of Serugh. A Song about Love*. Aide Inter-Monastères, 1992. FT by E. Khalifé-Hachem, in *Parole de l'Orient* 1 (1970): 281–99.

Love of Money: Hom. 103 (B III, 842–58). Abbreviated FT by Babakan in *Revue de l'Orient Chrétien* 19 (1914): 61–7.

Love of the World: unpublished.

Martyrion of St Stephen, Amid: unpublished.

Monks:—see Solitaries.

Nicaea, Council of: B VI, 231–54.

Poor, Complaint of: unpublished.

Priesthood: ed. with FT by M. Albert, in *Parole de l'Orient* 10 (1981/2): 54–65.

Priests: unpublished.

Repentance: Hom. 28–29 (B I, 646–66, 666–8).

Repentance: unpublished.

Rome, Conversion of by Peter: unpublished.

Sacrifices: unpublished.

Satan: unpublished.

Solitaries: Homs 137–8 (B IV, 818–36, 836–71).

Sophists: unpublished.

Supplication: unpublished.

Theatre (fragments): ed. with ET C. Moss, in *Le Muséon* 48 (1935), 87–112.

Three Baptisms: Hom. 7 (B I, 153–67). Abbreviated ET by S.P. Brock, in Finn, T. *Early Christian Baptism and the Catechumenate. West and East Syria*, 189–97. Collegeville, 1992.

I.2. *Madroshe/Sughyotho*

On Edessa: ed. with ET by Cureton, W. *Ancient Syriac Documents*, 107*–108*, 106–7. London, 1864; repr. 1967.

On the Soul: ed. with ET by S.P. Brock (see 29–37 in this volume).
Dialogue *sughyotho* attributed to Jacob: Sinful Woman and Satan; Church and Sion, Church and Synagogue; Joseph and Potiphar's Wife. For these, and other *sughyotho/madroshe* attributed to Jacob, see S.P. Brock, 'Jacob's forgotten *sughyotho*', 39–50 in this volume).

I.3. *Turgome* (Six Prose Homilies).

Editions:

Brock, S.P. *Shto turgome d-qadisho mor Ya'qub da-Srug malfono*. Monastery of St Ephrem, Holland, 1984.

Rilliet, F. *Jacques de Sarug. Six homélies festales en prose*. Patrologia Orientalis, 43; 1986.

Translations: Complete ET in Kollamparampil: I (Nativity) = pp. 128–36; II (Epiphany) = pp. 187–200; III (Great Fast) = pp. 231–45; IV (Palm Sunday) = pp. 261–77; V (Friday of the Passion) = pp. 278–91; VI (Resurrection) = pp. 318–28. Complete FT in Rilliet; and GT in Zingerle, P. *Sechs Homilie des heiligen Jacobs von Sarug*. Bonn/Aldenburg, 1887. Dutch tr. of I and II by K. den Biesen, in *Het christelijk Oosten* 48 (1996): 183–94, and 50 (1998): 167–83.

1.4. Lives of Saints (prose)

Daniel of Galash: unpublished. Summary in A.N. Palmer, "Sisters, fiancées, wives and mothers of Syrian Holy Men." In Lavenant, R., ed. *V Symposium Syriacum 1988*, 209–14. Orientalia Christiana Analecta, 236; 1990.

Hannina: unpublished. Summary in Nau, F. "Hagiographie syriaque: Histoire de Mar Hannina." *Revue de l'Orient Chrétien* 15 (1910): 62–4.

I.5. Letters (Forty three)

Edition: Olinder, G. *Iacobi Sarugensis Epistulae quotquot supersunt*. CSCO, II.45; Scr. Syri, 57; 1937.

Translation (French): Albert, M. *Les Lettres de Jacques de Saroug*. Patrimoine Syriaque, 3. Kaslik, 2004. Review by T. Bou Mansour, in *Parole de l'Orient* 34 (2009): 539–55.

Studies:

Albert, M. "A propos des citations scripturaires de la correspondence de Jacques de Saroug." *Studia Patristica* 35 (2001): 345–52.

Grill, S. "Der doppelte Stammbaum Christi nach Jacob von Sarug, Brief 23,6." *Texte und Untersuchungen* 133 (1987): 203–9.

Martin, J.-P.P. "Lettres de Jacques de Saroug aux moines du couvent de Mar Bassus." *Zeitschrift der deutschen morgenländischen Gesellschaft* 30 (1876) : 217–75.

Krüger, P. "Le caractère monophysite de la troisième lettre de Jacques de Saroug." *L'Orient Syrien* 6 (1961): 301–8.

Olinder, G. *The Letters of Jacob of Sarug. Comments on an Edition.* Lunds Universitets Årsskrift, N.F. Avd. 1, Bd 34, Nr 8. Lund, 1939.

Schröter, R. "Trostschreiben Jacob's von Sarug an die himjaritischen Christen." *Zeitschrift der deutschen morgenländischen Gesellschaft* 31 (1877): 360–405.

I.5. Liturgical Texts attributed to Jacob

(a) Anaphoras

Editions and translations: Three Anaphoras, ed. with LT by H.W. Codrington, in *Anaphorae Syriacae* II.i, 1–83. Rome, 1951. Ed. with ET of First Anaphora in Samuel, A.Y. *Anaphoras. The Book of Divine Liturgies*, 347–82. Lodi, NJ, 1991.

(b) Baptismal rite

Editions and translations: ed. with LT by Assemani, J.A. *Codex Liturgicus* II, 309–50; III,184–7. Rome, 1749–50. LT in Denzinger, H. *Ritus Orientalium* I, 334–50. Würzburg, 1863.

Photographic edition of Vatican Syr. 313, Paris Syr. 116–119, with FT: Mouhanna, A. *Les rites de l'initiation dans l'Église Maronite*. Orientalia Christiana Analecta, 212; 1980.

Study: Mouhanna, *Les rites de l'initiation*.

(c) Boʿawotho

Boʿawotho in the twelve-syllable metre are regularly ascribed to Jacob, and many are in fact excerpted, or adapted, from his *mimre*.

II. BIOGRAPHIES ETC. OF JACOB

There are a number of Lives (some in the form of panegyrics); details of manuscripts can be found in Vööbus, *Handschriftliche Überlieferung* I, pp. 1–16 (full title in III.2); these have been published as follows:

II.1. Short biography, ed. with LT by Abbeloos, J.B. *De vita et scriptis D. Jacobi...*, 311–4. Louvain, 1867, taken from British Library, Add. 12174 of AD 1196/7. This reads:

The father of this holy man was from Kurtam, on the Euphrates, His mother was barren, and her husband brought her to Mari of Barhadat,[5] and they prayed there. In accordance with God's will, he slept with her and she gave birth to a miraculous son. When he was three years old his parents brought him to pray there, on the Commemoration of the small child Mar Moqim. With a large crowd standing around, and when the House of God full of all sorts of peoples who had come to pray in the holy shrine, and the sanctuary was filled with priests, at the time when the Holy Spirit stirred to descend (at the Epiclesis) to sanctify the Body of our Life-giver, our Lord and our God and our Saviour, Jesus Christ, (Jacob) pushed his way through the people standing in the House of God and went up to the holy sanctuary; he stopped in front of the Table of Life, with the eyes of everyone in the Martyrion fixed on him, and the angel of the Lord stirred and descended, giving him the gift of God. He stretched out his hands and drank three handfuls—like Ezekiel eating from the scroll. And from that moment the Spirit of the Lord alighted upon him and he began to utter discourse that was out of the norm. He grew up in the Hawra of Serugh, and became periodeutes there. He composed numerous *mimre* there, and the Spirit called him and made him Pastor in the church of Batnan of Serugh. He wrote compositions, *turgome*, and also narratives and *sughyotho*. His teaching was glorious and unerring. His Lord was pleased and delighted with him. We find that his teaching was the equivalent of fifty prophets: the *mimre*

---

[5] Abbeloos translates 'to Mar Barhadath', but the *dolath* before Barhadath makes that impossible.

numbered 763. The last *mimro* that he composed, but did not complete, was on Mary and Golgotha.

Mar Jacob lived in the time of Mar Severus, whom he went to visit and to receive a blessing from him, He went there in the company of many bishops from the entire Orient. Time is too short for us to recount his way of life, right up to the day of his death, his modesty, sanctity, his purity and asceticism, his vigils and labour, his toil and ministry, his tears and his groans, his love, his virtue and his prayers. May his prayer and supplication be for us a protective wall and refuge at all times, for eternal ages.

II.2. Short notice, ed. with LT in Assemani, *Bibliotheca Orientalis* I, 206–9, taken from Vatican Syr. 37, dated 1626/7. This reads:

The holy Mar Jacob the Teacher, the Flute of the Holy Spirit and the Lyre of the faithful Church, was from the village of Kurtam on the river Euphrates. He was the child of a vow by his faithful parents, who were barren. After he was born, when he was three years old, his mother was present at one of the Feasts of our Lord, and at the moment in the Anaphora of the descent of the Holy Spirit upon the Mysteries, the holy child got down from his mother's arms pushed his way through the people and went to the Holy Table where he partook of three drafts of the Holy Spirit. From then on he began to pour forth *mimre* and teachings. Once the bishops heard of him they came along to investigate him; they instructed him to utter a *mimro* on the Chariot which Ezekiel saw. He began to utter 'O Exalted One who is seated upon the Chariot of the Heavenly Beings...'. They then told him to set down in writing his teaching in the Church, so he began to compose *mimre* and teachings in the Church when he was 22. Subsequently, when he was sixty seven and a half years old, he became bishop in the town of Serugh, this being 830 of the Greeks (= AD 518/9), in the 519th year after the coming of Christ. Having filled the Church with life-giving doctrine and having ... the entire world with his teaching and glorious , he departed to his Lord. He was buried with honour in his town of Serugh in the year 833, on the 29th November (= AD 521). The total years of his life were 70, 67 and a half of which were before he became bishop, and two and a half while he was bishop.

II.3. Biography in Mardin Orth. 256, dated 1665. This was described by Vööbus in "Eine unbekannte Biographie des Ja'qob von Sarug," *Zeitschrift für Kirchengeschichte* 23 (1974): 399–405. This informative text certainly deserves to be published; according to Vööbus, it alone could be considered to be a proper biography.

II.4. Panegyric, ed. with LT in Abbeloos, *De vita et scriptis D. Jacobi...*, 24–85, taken from Vatican Syr. 117 of 12th/13th cent. Assemani attributed it to George, a disciple of Jacob, but this cannot be correct; In other manuscripts it is attributed to a Habbib or to Patriarch bar Shushan. The text of a different manuscript (Paris Syr. 177) was edited (with GT) by Krüger, P. "Ein bislang unbekannter sermo über Leben und Werk des Jacob von Sarug." *Oriens Christianus* 56 (1972): 80–111. Vööbus, *Handschriftliche Überlieferung*, I, 8–13, lists a number of other witnesses to the text.

II.5. Another long Panegyric, by Sa'id bar Sabuni (d. 1095) was edited by Krüger (from Paris Syr. 177) in "Ein zweiter anonyme memra über Jacob von Sarug." *Oriens Christianus* 56 (1972): 112–49. Vööbus, *Handschriftliche Überlieferung*, I, 13–16, lists several considerably earlier manuscripts, among which Chicago, Oriental Institute A. 12,008, of the 12th/13th century, is probably correct naming the author as Sa'id bar Sabuni.

II.6. The late Mar Philoxenos Yuhanon Dolabani (d. 1969) published **a short biography of Jacob** based on earlier Syriac sources, under the title *Swodo mphaygono 'al ḥayyaw w-malphonutheh d-qadisho Mar Ya'qob Malphono*. Mardin, 1952.

III. STUDIES (SELECT)

III.1. General Introductions

Abbeloos, J.B. *De vita et scriptis D. Jacobi Batnarum Sarugi in Mesopotamia episcopi*. Louvain, 1867.

Assemani, J.S. *Bibliotheca Orientalis* I, 283–340. Rome, 1719, and reprints.

Barsoum, I.A. *The Scattered Pearls. A History of Syriac Literature and Sciences*, 255–61. Piscataway, NJ, ²2003.

Baumstark, A. *Geschichte der syrischen Literatur*, 148–58. Bonn, 1922.
Graffin, F. "Jacques de Saroug." *Dictionnaire de Spiritualité* 8 (1974): 56–60.
Hage, W. "Jakob von Sarug." *Theologische Realenzyklopädie* 16 (1987): 470–74.
Lange, C. "Jakob von Sarug." In Klein, W., ed. *Syrische Kirchenväter*, 217–27. Stuttgart, 2004.
Ortiz de Urbina, I. *Patrologia Syriaca*, 104–9. Rome, ²1965.
Rilliet, F. "Jakob von Sarug." *Realenzyklopädie für Antike und Christentum* 16 (1994): 1217–27.
Tisserant, E. "Jacques de Saroug." *Dictionnaire de Théologie Catholique* 8:1 (1924): 300–5.

III.2. Monographs

Alwan, Kh. *Anthropologie de Jacques de Saroug: l'homme 'microcosme', avec une bibliographie générale raisonnée*. Diss. Kaslik, 1988. [See also under 3, below].
Bou Mansour, T. *La théologie de Jacques de Saroug*. I, *Création, anthropologie, ecclésiologie et sacrements*. Kaslik, 1993; II, *Christologie, Trinité, eschatologie, méthode exégétique et théologique*. Kaslik, 2000.
Kollamparampil, T. *Salvation in Christ according to Jacob of Serugh: a Exegetico-Theological Study of the Homilies of Jacob of Serugh on the Feasts of our Lord*. Bangalore/Rome, 2001.
Puthuparampil, J. *The Mariological Thought of Mar Jacob of Serugh (451–521)*. Moran Etho, 25. Kottayam, 2005.
Sony, B. *La doctrine de Jacques de Saroug sur la création et l'anthropologie*. Diss. Rome, 1989. [See also under 3, below].
Vööbus, A. *Handschriftliche Überlieferung der Memre-Dichtung des Ja'qob von Serug*, I–IV. CSCO, 344–5, 421–2 = Subs. 39–40, 60–61; 1973, 1980.

III.3. Articles on specific topics

Albert, M. "Jacques de Saroug et le Magistère." *Parole de l'Orient* 17 (1992): 61–71.
Alwan, Kh. "L'Homme, le 'microcosme' chez Jacques de Saroug." *Parole de l'Orient* 13 (1986): 51–77.
___. "Le *remzo* selon la pensée de Jacques de Saroug." *Parole de l'Orient* 15 (1988/9): 91–106.

Alwan, Kh. "Était-il mortel our immortel, l'homme, avant le péché pour Jacques de Saroug?" *Orientalia Christiana Periodica* 55 (1989): 5–31.

Black, M. "The Gospel text of Jacob of Serug." *Journal of Theological Studies* NS 2 (1951): 57–63.

Blum, J.G. "Zum Bau von Abschnitten in Memre von Jakob von Sarug." In *III Symposium Syriacum*, 307–21. Orientalia Christiana Analecta, 221; 1983.

Bou Mansour, T. "L'Eucharistie chez Jacques de Saroug." *Parole de l'Orient* 17 (1992): 37–59.

———. "Die christologie des Jakob von Sarug." In Grillmeier, A. (ed. Th. Hainthaler). *Jesus der Christus im Glauben der Kirche*, II.3, 449–99. Freiburg, 2002.

Brock, S.P. "Baptismal themes in the writings of Jacob of Serugh." In *II Symposium Syriacum*, 325–47. Orientalia Christiana Analecta, 205; 1978.

———. "The Wedding Feast of Blood: an unusual aspect of John 19:34 in Syriac tradition." *The Harp* 6:2 (1993): 121–34.

———. "An extract from Jacob of Serugh in the East Syrian Hudra." *Orientalia Christiana Periodica* 55 (1989): 339–43. [Turgomo on Resurrection].

———. "Dieu Amour et Amour de Dieu chez Jacques de Saroug." In *Dieu miséricorde, Dieu d'Amour*, 173–83. Patrimoine Syriaque, Colloque VIII. Antelias, 2002.

Carr, E. "L'Hodie nei sermoni ritmici di Giacobbe di Serug per le grande feste." *Ecclesia Orans* 16 (1999): 17–28.

Connolly, R.H. "Jacob of Serug and the Diatessaron." *Journal of Theological Studies* 8 (1907): 581–90.

Cramer, W. "Irrtum und Lüge. Zum Urteil des Jakob von Sarug über Reste paganer Religion und Kultur." *Jahrbuch für Antike und Christentum* 23 (1980): 96–107.

den Biesen, K. "Giacomo di Sarug predicatore." In Vergani, E., and S. Chialà, eds. *La tradizione cristiana Siro-occidentale (V–VII secolo)*, 109–27. Milan, 2007.

Golitzin, A. "The image and glory of God in Jacob of Serugh's homily 'On that Chariot that Ezekiel the prophet saw.'" *St Vladimir's Seminary Theological Quarterly* 47:3/4 (2003): 323–64. Reprinted in *Scrinium* (St Petersburg) 3 (2007): 180–212.

Graffin, F. "Le thème de la perle chez Jacques de Saroug." *L'Orient Syrien* 12 (1967): 355–70.

Guinan, M. "Where are the dead? Purgatory and immediate retribution in James of Serugh." In Ortiz de Urbina, I., ed. *[I] Symposium Syriacum*, 541–50. Orientalia Christiana Analecta, 197; 1974.

Harvey, S.A. "Interior decorating: Jacob of Serugh on Mary's preparation for the Incarnation." *Studia Patristica* 411 (2006): 23–28.

___. "Bride of Blood, Bride of Light: biblical women as images of the Church in Jacob of Serugh." In Kiraz, G, ed. *Malphono w-Rabo d-Malphone. Studies in Honor of Sebastian P. Brock*, 177–204. Gorgias Eastern Christian Studies, 3. Piscataway, NJ, 2008.

Jansma, T. "The credo of Jacob of Serugh: a return to Nicaea and Constantinople." *Nederlandsch Archiev voor Kerkgeschiedenis* 44 (1960): 18–36.

___. "Encore le credo de Jacques de Saroug." *L'Orient Syrien* 10 (1965): 75–88, 193–236, 331–70, 475–510.

___. "Die Christologie Jakobs von Serugh und ihre Abhängigkeit Ephraems des Syrers." *Le Muséon* 78 (1965): 5–46.

Kollamparampil, T. "Adam-Christ complementarity and the economy of salvation in Jacob of Serugh." *The Harp* 13 (2000): 147–70.

Konat, J. "Christological insights in Jacob of Serugh's typology as reflected in his memre." *Ephemerides Theologicae Lovanienses* 77 (~2001): 46–72.

___. "Typological exegesis in the metrical homilies of Jacob of Serugh." *Parole de l'Orient* 31 (2006): 109–21.

Krüger, P. "Die kirchliche Zugehörigkeit Jacobs von Serugh im Lichte der handschriftliche Überlieferung seiner Vita unter besonderer Berücksichtigung der Pariser Handschrift 177." *Ostkirchliche Studien* 13 (1964): 15–32.

___. "Zwei Bemerkungen über die Privatbeichte bei Jakob von Serugh." *Ostkirchliche Studien* 19 (1970): 44–5.

___. "Neues über die Frage der Konfessionszugehörigkeit Jakobs von Serugh." In *Wegzeichen. Festgabe ... H.M. Biedermann*, 245–253. Würzburg, 1971.

Lane, D.J. "'There is no need of turtle doves or young pigeons' (Jacob of Sarug). Quotations and non-quotations of Leviticus in selected Syriac writers." In ter Haar Romeny, R.B., ed. *The*

Peshitta. Its use in Literature and Liturgy. Third Peshitta Symposium, 143–58. Leiden, 2006.

Martin, J.-P.P. "Un évêque poète au Ve et au VIe siècles, ou Jacques de Saroug: sa vie, son temps, ses oeuvres, ses croyances." *Revue des Sciences Ecclésiastiques* IV.3 (1876): 309–52, 385–419.

Menze, V. "Jacob of Serugh, John of Tella and Paul of Edessa: ecclesiastical politics in Osrhoene 519–522." In Kiraz G., ed. *Malphono w-Rabo d-Malphone. Studies in Honor of Sebastian P. Brock*, 421–38. Gorgias Eastern Christian Studies, 3. Piscataway, NJ, 2008.

Morrison, C. "David's opening speech (I Sam 17:34–37a) according to Jacob of Serugh." In Kiraz G., ed. *Malphono w-Rabo d-Malphone. Studies in Honor of Sebastian P. Brock*, 477–96. Gorgias Eastern Christian Studies 3; Piscataway NJ, 2008.

Palmer, A.N. "What Jacob actually wrote about Ephrem." In Gerhards, A., and C. Leonhard, eds. *Jewish and Christian Liturgy: New Insights*, 145–65. Leiden, 2007.

Papoutsakis, M. "Formulaic language in the metrical homilies of Jacob of Serugh." In Lavenant, R., ed. *Symposium Syriacum VII*, 445–51. Orientalia Christiana Analecta 256; 1998.

Peeters, P. "Jacques de Saroug appartient-il à la secte monophysite?" *Analecta Bollandiana* 66 (1948): 134–98.

Rilliet, F. "Rhétorique et style à l'époque de Jacques de Saroug." In Drijvers, H.J.W., and others, eds., *IV Symposium Syriacum*, 289–95. Orientalia Christiana Analecta 229; 1987.

___. "La métaphore du chemin dans la sotériologie de Jacques de Saroug." *Studia Patristica* 25 (1993): 324–31.

___. "Une victime du tournant des études syriaques à la fin du XIXe siècle: Retrospective sur Jacques de Saroug dans la science occidentale." *Aram* 5 (1993): 465–80.

___. "Deux homéliaires sarougiens du VIe siècle à la Bibliothèque Vaticane." in *Miscellanea Bibliothecae Apostolicae Vaticanae* (Studi et Testi 416; 2003), 293–337.

Samir, Kh. "Un exemple des contacts culturels entre les Églises syriaques et arabes: Jacques de Saroug das la tradition arabe." In Lavenant, R., ed. *III Symposium Syriacum*, 213–45. Orientalia Christiana Analecta 221; 1983.

Scopello, M. "Jacques de Sarough et l'Exegèse de l'Âme." *Deuxième journée d'études coptes*, 130–6. Cahiers de la Bibliothèque Copte, 3; 1986 [On Hom. VI against the Jews].

Sony, B.M.B. "La méthode exégétique de Jacques de Saroug." *Parole de l'Orient* 9 (1979/80): 67–103.

___. "L'Anthropologie de Jacques de Saroug." *Parole de l'Orient* 12 (1984/5): 153–85.

Sony, B.M.B. "La dette commune (*Hawbat gawo*)" [in Jacob]. In *Patrimoine Syriaque, Colloque* IV, 111–36. Antélias, 1997.

Thekeparampil, J. "Simon chez Ephrem et Jacques de Saroug." In *Saint Ephrem, un poète pour notre temps*, 109–23. Patrimoine Syriaque, Colloque XI. Antelias, 2007.

___. "St Peter in the homilies of Jacob of Serugh." *Parole de l'Orient* 31 (2006): 123–32.

Uhlig, S. "Dersan des Ya'qob von Sarug." *Aethiopica* 2 (1999): 7–52.

Wurmbrand, M. "Dersana, une homélie éthiopienne attribuée à Jacques de Saroug." *L'Orient Syrien* 8 (1963): 343–94.

Zingerle, P. "Über Jakob von Sarug und seine Typologie." *Zeitschrift für katholische Theologie* 11 (1887): 92–108; FT by Forthomme, B. "La typologie de Jacques de Saroug." In *Splendeur du Carmel*, 50–63. Beirut, 1996.

III.4. For further bibliography

A very full bibliography on Jacob was provided by Alwan, Kh. "Bibliographie générale raisonnée de Jacques de Saroug." *Parole de l'Orient* 13 (1986): 313–83. Subsequent bibliography can be found in Brock, S.P. *Syriac Studies: a classified bibliography (1960–1990)*. Kaslik, 1996, and the subsequent five-yearly updates published in *Parole de l'Orient* 23 (1998) for 1991–1995, 29 (2004) for 1996–2000, and 33 (2008) for 2001–2005.